Training Manual
Fine Finish – HVLP & Conventional spraying

Paint tech training academy
www.painttechtrainingacademy.co.uk
27/03/2021
6 X 9

Aim

Our aim is to give decorators the skills and knowledge needed to allow them to successfully spray using HVLP and conventional systems in their business.

Course objectives

1. Be able to assemble the parts of a HVLP system.

2. Establish air change requirements in a confined space.

3. Understand the suitability of a surface for spraying.

4. Understand Health and Safety when spraying.

5. Be able to mask and protect surfaces properly.

6. Be able to prepare the paint correctly.

7. Understand how to use the controls on a HVLP gun.

8. Be able to correctly spray a range of surfaces.

9. Understand how to use a dry film thickness gauge.

10. Be able to troubleshoot the equipment.

11. Be able to shut down and store the equipment.

Spraying systems

There are a number of spraying systems on the market for the decorator to use. Each one has its own advantages and disadvantages. Never does one system do everything really well.

The four main systems on the market are:

Airless

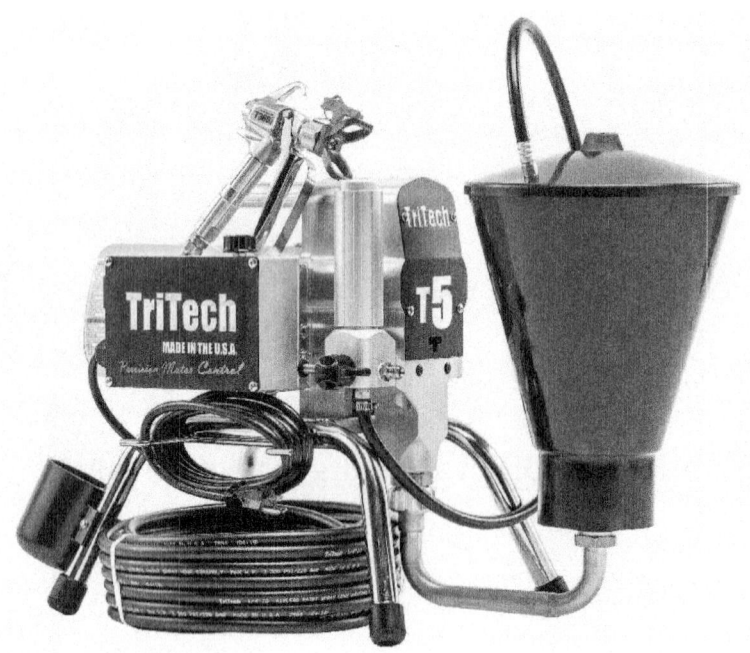

This is very fast.

Air assisted airless

This is also fast and has a high-end finish.

Conventional

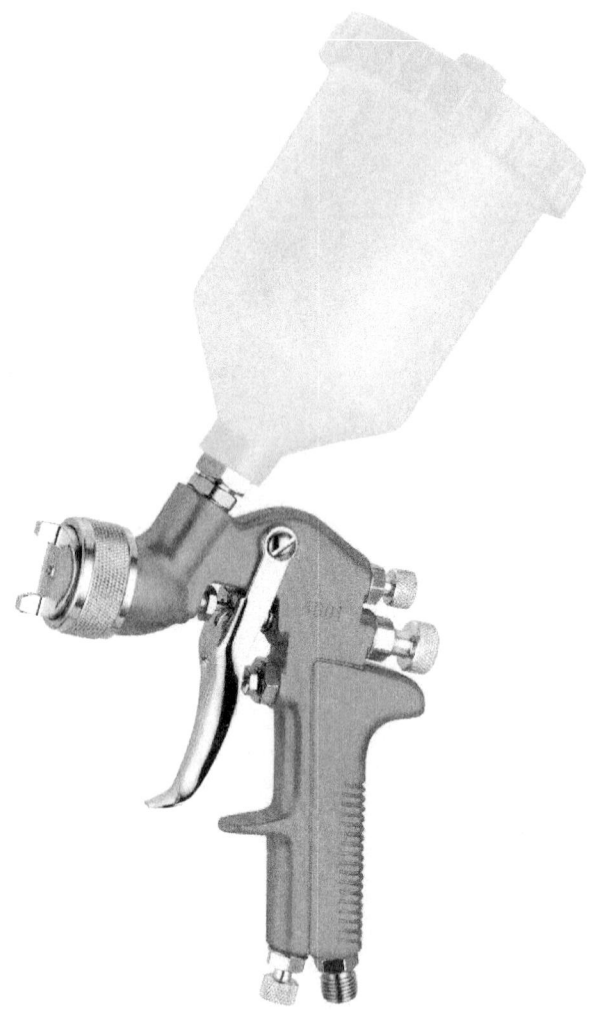

Used with a compressor, this is a low-cost system.

HVLP – High Volume Low Pressure

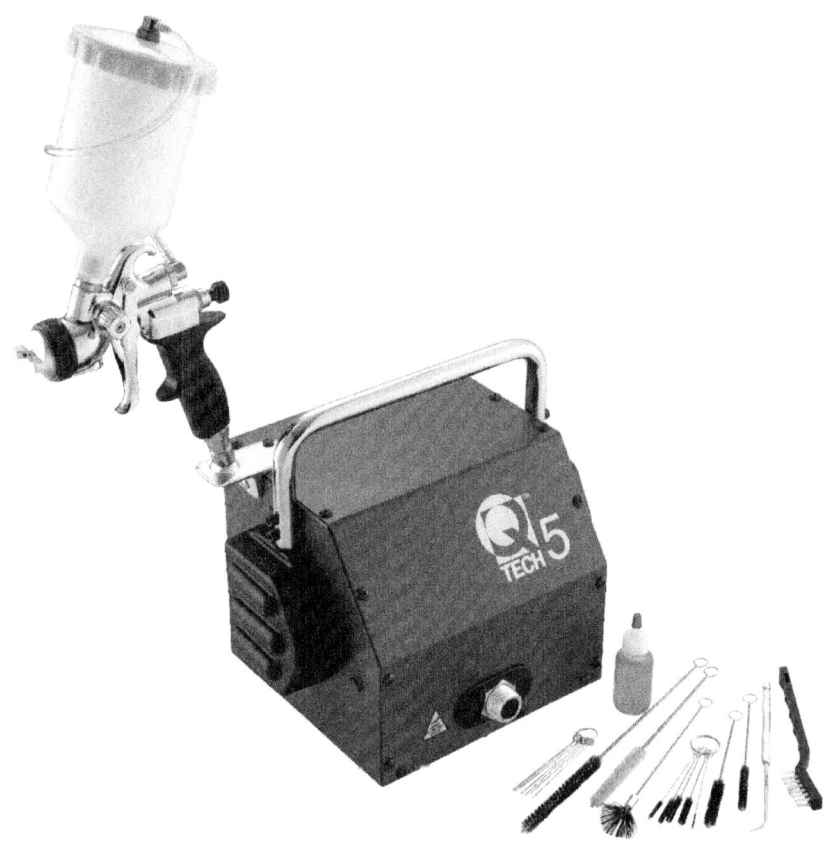

A fine finish with very little overspray, it is also very portable.

Advantages and disadvantages

Each system has a reason to use it and a place where it is not suitable.

Airless

This is amazingly fast and is good for large areas where production is the main criteria. For example, large areas of plaster surfaces and block walls.

It is not for a fine finish. For example, you could not spray a car with an airless system, the finish would just not be good enough.

Air Assisted Airless

This is mainly used in joinery manufacturing workshops. A proper air assisted airless set up consists of a compressor and an airless pump. An air hose runs from the compressor and a fluid hose runs from the pump. The gun is specially designed to take both hoses.

The airless pump will deliver thicker paints and the air flow softens the atomised paint giving you a fine finish. The set up can be used on site but it is cumbersome.

The equipment is also very expensive. For example, a gun can cost £600. On site the finish advantage is outweighed by these factors.

Conventional

This is a compressor and spray gun. The advantage is that it can be bought cheaply, and you can achieve a fine finish with it. This is what most car sprayers would use when respraying a car. Some decorators are using this set up to spray uPVC windows, due to the low cost of the equipment.

This disadvantage is that it will only spray thin materials and you will get quite a bit of overspray due to the pressure that you are spraying at. The compressor can be quite heavy to transport on site.

HVLP (High Volume Low Pressure)

The advantage of this system is that it is both very light and portable and sprays at a very low pressure meaning that you get very little overspray.

The disadvantage is that the equipment is very expensive, you need to spend over a grand for a decent system. It will only spray thin products too. Standard satin paints that are designed to be brushed and rolled are very difficult to spray with HVLP.

Here are examples of ideal surfaces for each system

Airless

This would be an ideal job, spraying emulsion on a large blockwork area.

Air Assisted Airless

Spraying manufactured windows with a specialist product such as Renner primer.

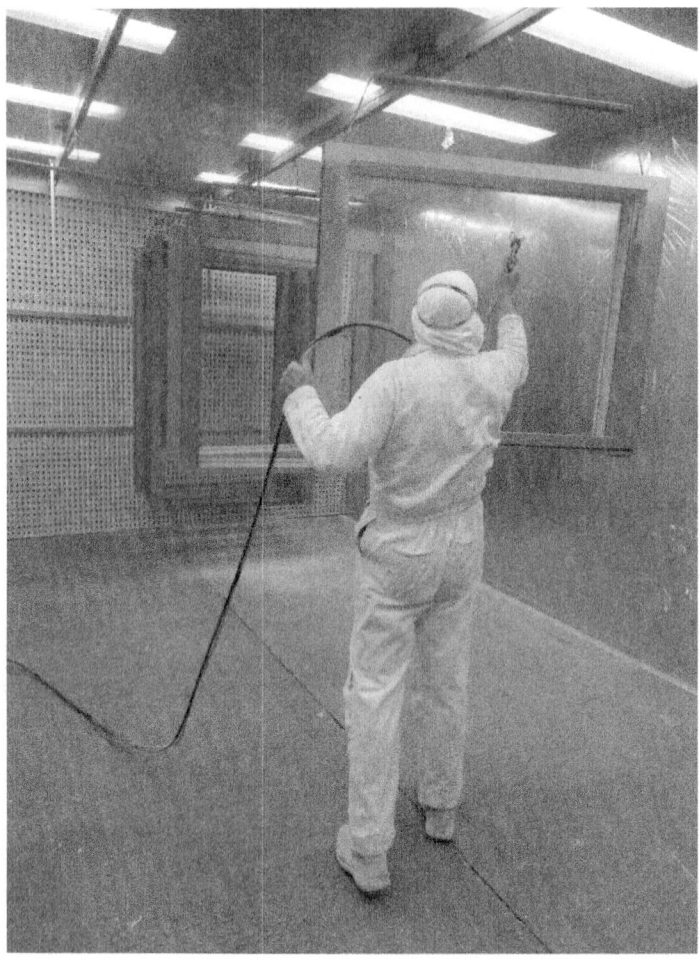

Conventional

Spraying a car in a spray booth (to overcome the overspray) is an ideal job for a conventional spray gun.

HVLP (High Volume Low Pressure)

You can dial the spray fan down to a spot with HVLP and there is very little overspray. With the right type of paint HVLP would be ideal to spray spindles.

Assemble the parts of a HVLP system

There are three parts to a HVLP system

The Turbine

You can see how small it is, the screw fitting on the front is for the air hose to screw onto. The box on the side is the filter.

The gun

There are **three** types of gun, gravity feed (shown) suction feed and pressure feed (with a pressure pot). We will discuss this later when we look at conventional spray guns.

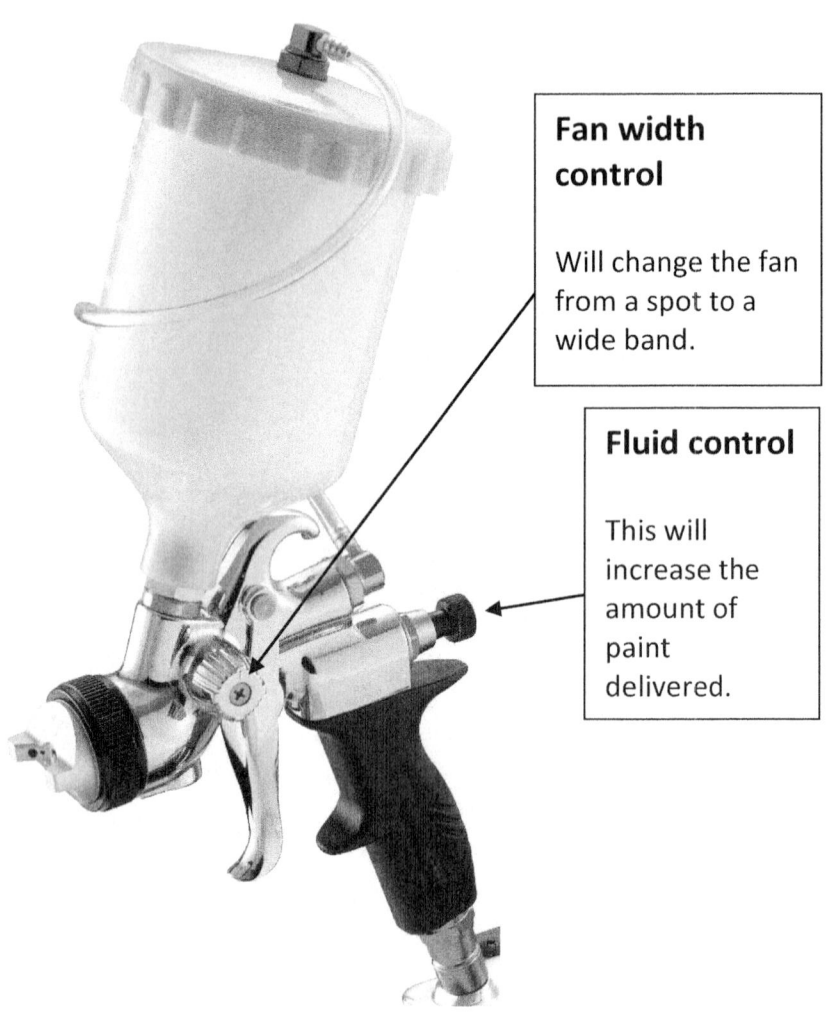

Fan width control

Will change the fan from a spot to a wide band.

Fluid control

This will increase the amount of paint delivered.

The hose

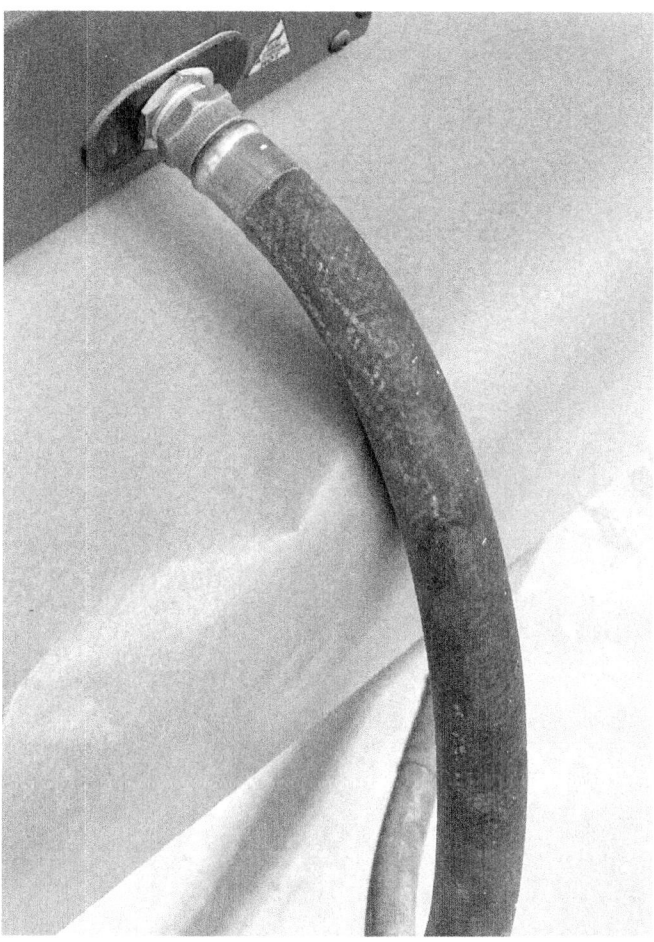

The hose to the HVLP is quite stiff and inflexible. The part which attaches to the turbine gets **very hot** so do not touch it or unscrew it until it has cooled down, it will burn you.

The whip hose

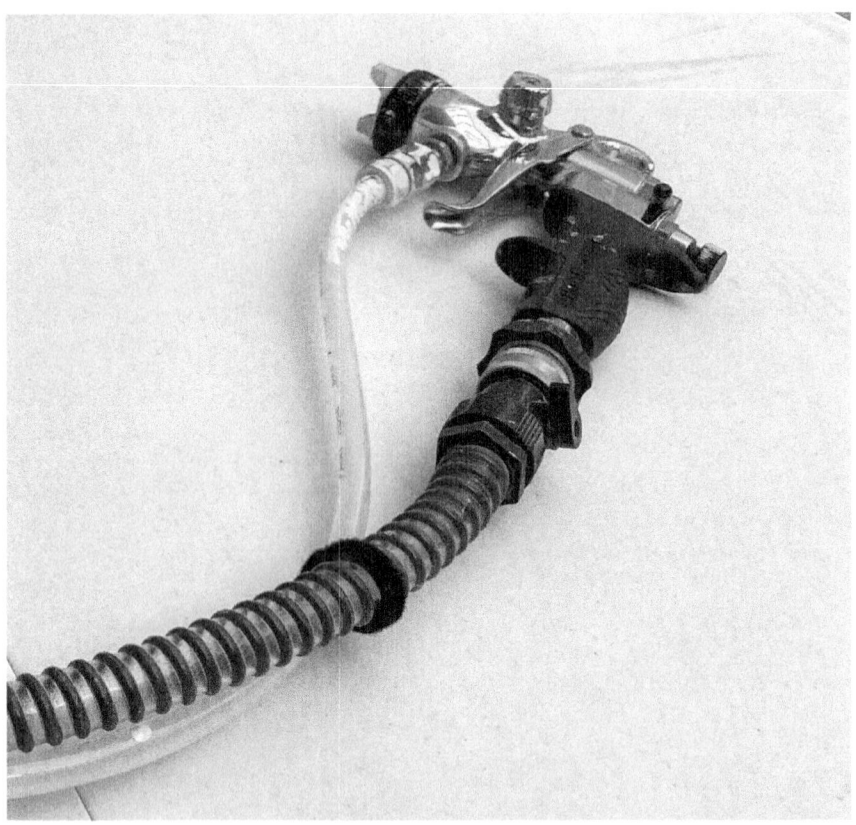

The whip hose is a short length of flexible hose which makes to gun easier to use. Here you can see it attached to the gun.

Tip sets

A tip set for most HVLP systems is made up of three parts as shown in the picture. The fluid tip, the fluid needle and the air cap. These are quite expensive to buy but you will get a tip set when you buy your HVLP.

The size of the tip is measured in mm with typical sizes being 1.3mm, 1.5mm and 1.8mm.

A good all-round tip to use is the 1.5mm. Wagner and Graco use a number system with relates to the mm sizes as follows.

#2 – 1.0mm – Fine, stains and dyes
#3 – 1.3mm – Fine to medium - lacquers etc
#4 – 1.5mm – Medium – Most paints
#5 – 1.8mm – High – Emulsions

Do not overthink the tip sizes, you will find that you will use the same tip size for most of your work, you can control the fluid output using the fluid control to reduce the amount of paint delivered. You will not be spraying thicker paints through the HVLP.

Establish air change requirements in a confined space

What does this mean? If you are spraying in a room then you need to establish good ventilation. Open a window for example.

If you are spraying water-based paints such as Tikkurila Akvi then if you are wearing a mask and you vacate the room once you gave finished spraying, then that is fine.

If you are spraying in a confined space with no ventilation, then you will have to use a portable extraction system.

Suitability of a surface for spraying

Before a surface is sprayed it must be checked and then prepared.

A surface will fall into 2 main categories
Porous
Non-porous

Porous surfaces, such as new wood and bare plaster are easy to spray because they will absorb the paint and it is difficult to overload the surface and get runs. They need to be sealed though with a suitable primer, thinned so that it penetrates the surface.

Non-porous surfaces, such as glass, tiles and plastic must be degreased before painting. Plastic can be very finely abraded with a "Scotch Brite" pad and glass and tiles need a specialist adhesion primer.

Metal surfaces need to be free from corrosion and if new they will need to be primed with a suitable metal primer. Steel needs a rust inhibiting primer.

Health and safety when spraying

When you are spraying you need to wear a mask. There are two types of mask, particle, and vapour.

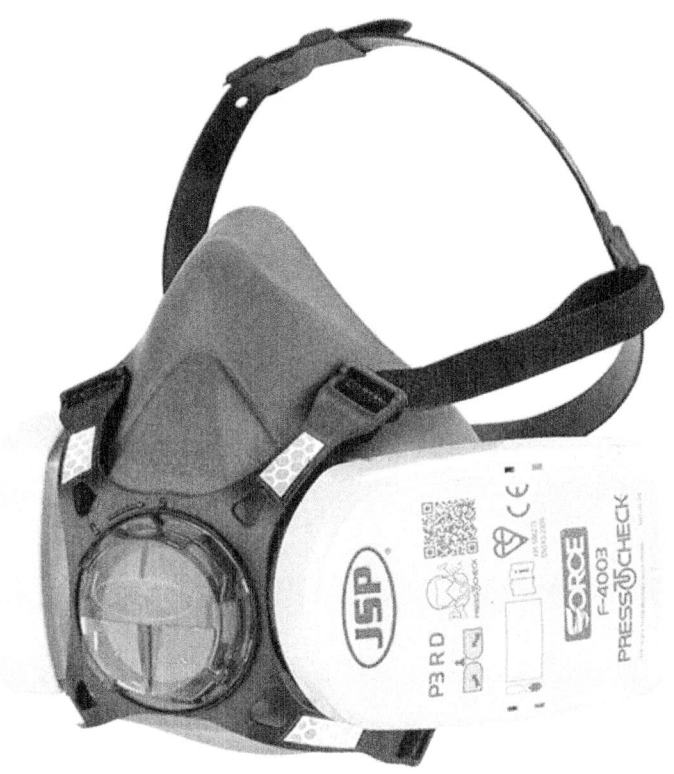

Particle mask

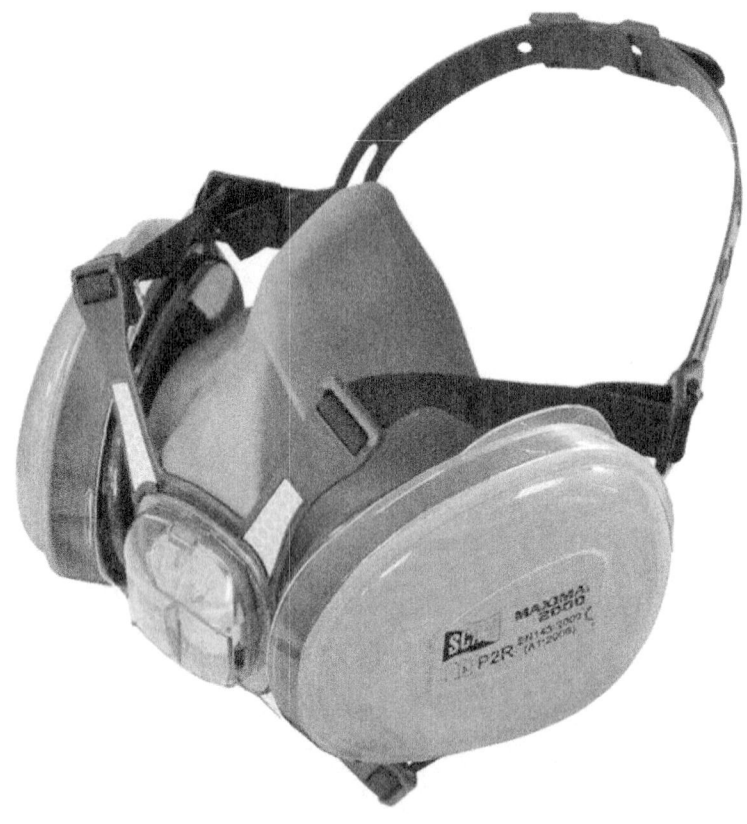

Vapour mask

How the rating system works

P1 dust masks

These are recommended for workplaces with low levels of dust. They are ideal where you are sanding with moderate dust levels.

P2 dust mask

This is better than a P1 and offer protection against moderate levels of dust.

P3 dust mask

Better than P1 & P2 and used where there is a high concentration of dust.

An A1 dust mask will protect against organic gases.

Obviously an A1P3 mask will protect against both vapour and particles and is what we would use when spraying.

Mask and protect surfaces properly

Masking is an important topic if you are a sprayer. Masking is a course in itself. We have developed an online masking course that is worth checking out.

The three most commonly used masking materials are tape, paper and film.

Masking tape comes in different widths and types.

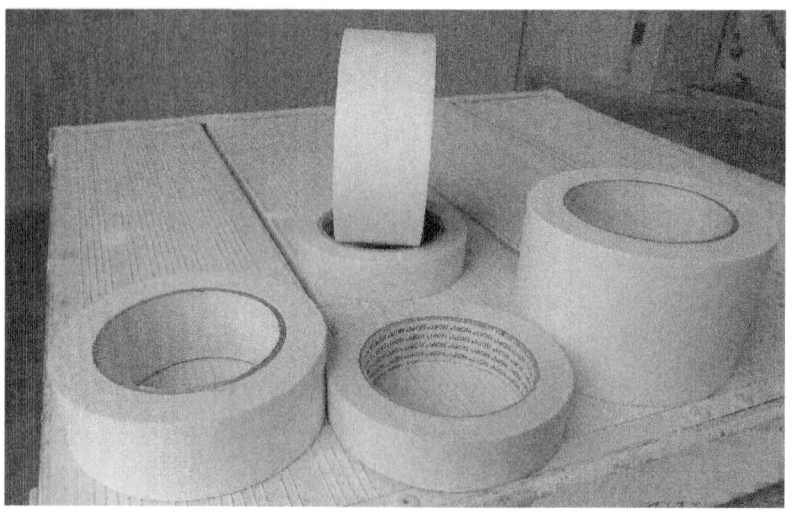

The two main tapes are standard masking tape and precision tape.

Standard tape is cheap to buy but is not great to use. It will dry onto the surface very quickly and be difficult to remove, it will not give you a sharp line and the paint will bleed very easily. It is however good for certain jobs such putting on your hand masker, taping light switches and sockets and also taping off the carpet.

Precision tape is for getting a sharp line. For example if you have finished the skirtings in white and the wall is going to be finished in a dark blue then you will need to tape the skirtings off in a precision tape to get that amazing sharp line.

Paper comes in various widths and the two I use the most are 12" and 6" widths. The narrower paper is useful for taping off skirtings and door casings while the wider paper is good for masking off bathrooms and kitchens.

Plastic film is great for when you need to completely protect a surface from paint, examples include kitchens, baths, tiled areas and windows.

Prepare the paint correctly

Paint is an interesting topic when talking to painters. You would think that they would be complete experts in paint however the opposite is usually true. Especially when they start to try and spray paint.

When you go to your paint supplier and look at the paint on the shelves then most of the paint has been designed to be brushed and rolled because this is the biggest market in this country.

Everyone assumes that a paint that is designed to be brushed will also be good to spray but this is not the case. If you are serious about getting into spraying, then you need to do some research and experiment with some new products.

Wet film thickness and dry film thickness

When you apply a coat of paint to a surface it will be a certain thickness, typically 50 microns (1000 microns is a millimetre).

This is the wet film thickness (WFT), and this can be measured using a wet film thickness comb. In some cases, this a really important measurement for example when applying intumescent paint. It is good to understand what a coat of paint measures.

Most people think if a coat of paint as something that is applied once by brush. This will be about 50 microns when wet. When it dries back it will be about half the thickness depending on the solids content of the paint.

This is the dry film thickness (DFT).

Solids content of paint

What is this then? The solid content is what is left on the surface once the paint has dried. So, for example if a satin paint has a solids content of 50% then it will be 100 microns when wet and 50 microns when dry.

Two coats would be 100 microns when dry.

When you look at the data sheet for most decorative paints, they are disappointingly low. Usually between 30% and 40% depending on the brand.

Getting the consistency right

Before you can spray a paint through a HVLP system the paint needs to be single cream consistency. This is quite thin for most decorative paints. You need to be careful that you don't over thin the paint otherwise you will need to give the surface many coats to get the correct build.

Data sheets will advise you how much you can thin paints, if you are thinning too much then it will be worth finding another product.

Paints for spraying

Some paints have been formulated to spray. Two examples are Renner 643 primer and Tikkurila Akvi.

These paints are ready to spray out of the tin and have a good solids content and build when sprayed. Greater in many cases that their thicker brush and roll counterparts.

How to use the controls on a HVLP gun

There are 2 controls on a HVLP gun, these are:

Fan control

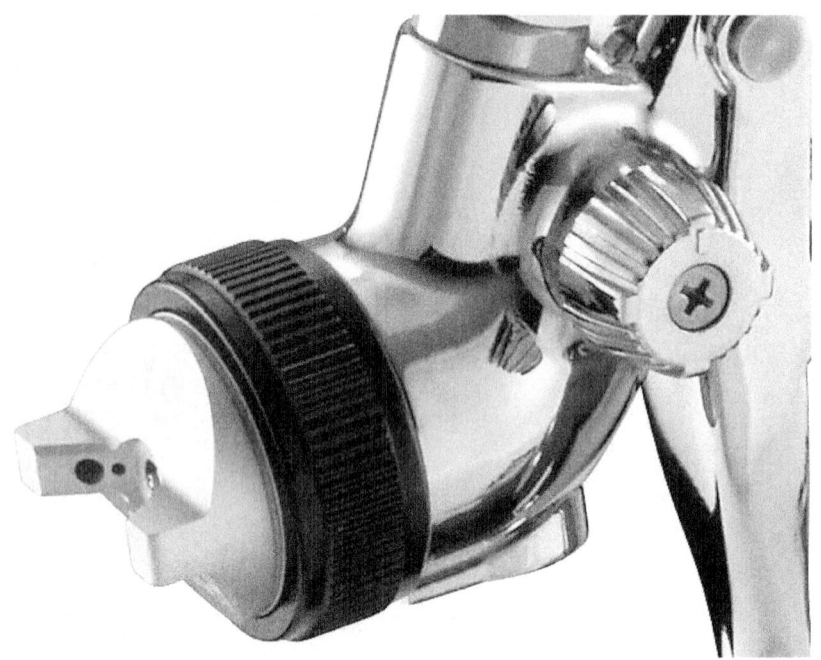

This is the fan control on the Q-tech Q5 gun. You can see that it is a dial on the side of the gun. It will only do a quarter turn. When the arrow is pointing forward then the fan width is set to a spot. When you dial it back so that the arrow points up (as shown in the picture) then that is a wide fan.

Because it is only a quarter turn it means that it is very sensitive. A slight turn will alter the fan width a lot.

Fluid control

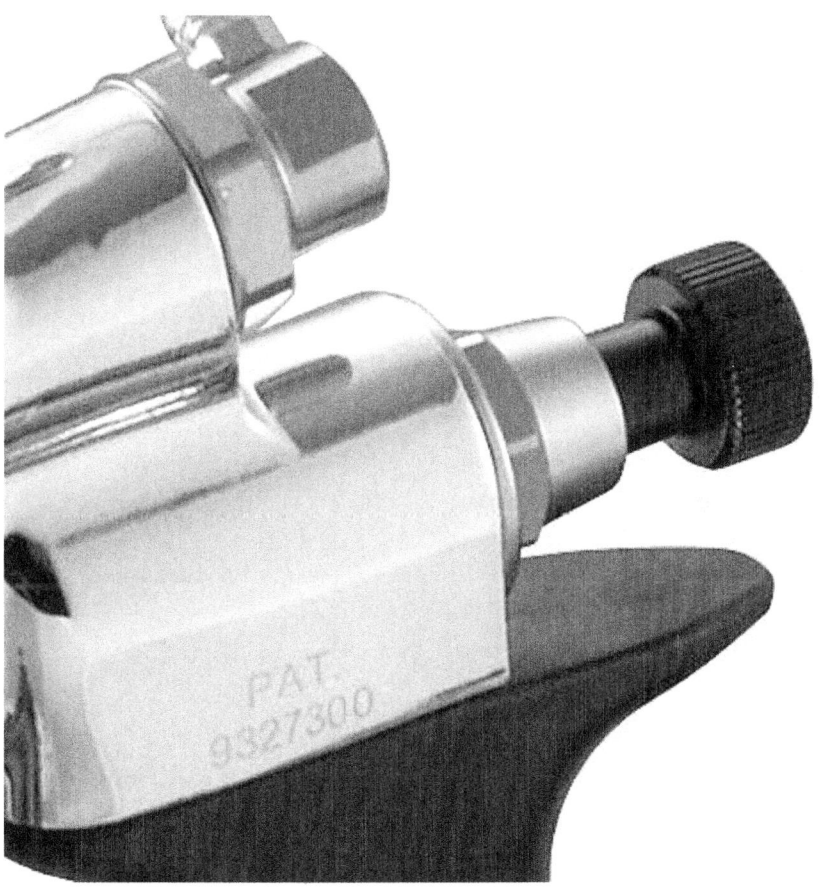

The fluid control sets the amount of paint that will flow through the fluid tip. If you screw it all the way in (turn clockwise) then this will completely close off the paint.

Then as you screw it out (anti clockwise) this will allow more and more paint to be allowed through the fluid tip. This dial is less sensitive than the fan width so I would do two complete 360 degree turns and then try it to see how much more paint you have.

There is a relationship between the two controls. If you are only spraying a narrow line, then you do not need much paint, so you dial the fluid control in.

As you widen the fan you will need more paint because the same amount of paint is spread over a wider area. You get quite quick at this and you will only have to set it up once if you are spraying a similar area all day.

Spray a range of surfaces

You will spray a range of surfaces including, skirtings, a door, a sample panel, spindles, a plastic chair, and a window. Each surface will need a certain setting on the gun to get the best results.

The two extremes are the door and the spindles. The door will need a wide fan with plenty of paint coming out and a spindle will need a narrow fan with less fluid.

We will also spray a range of materials that are ideal to be sprayed using HVLP systems.

Conventional spray systems

Once you have used the HVLP system and mastered the controls on the gun then you will be able to use a conventional spray gun as well because the controls are exactly the same.

There are a few advantages to using a conventional spray system.

1. It's cheaper to get set up. You can buy a compressor and spray gun for around £200. Ok these are not the best or state of the art, but they will get you going, and you can make some money with them.

2. You can spray at a range of pressures and spray thicker materials. The compressor allows you to control the pressure that you spray at. This means that you can dial it down to a low pressure to reduce overspray or you can have a higher pressure to atomise slightly thicker materials.

3. If you decide to set up an air assisted airless system you are halfway there, especially if you bought yourself a decent compressor like the Gentilin.

The Gentilin compressor, available from Sprayman UK. You have to admit, this is a pretty cool compressor and it performs great as well.

The spray guns

As with the HVLP systems there are 3 types of spray gun.

The gravity feed gun

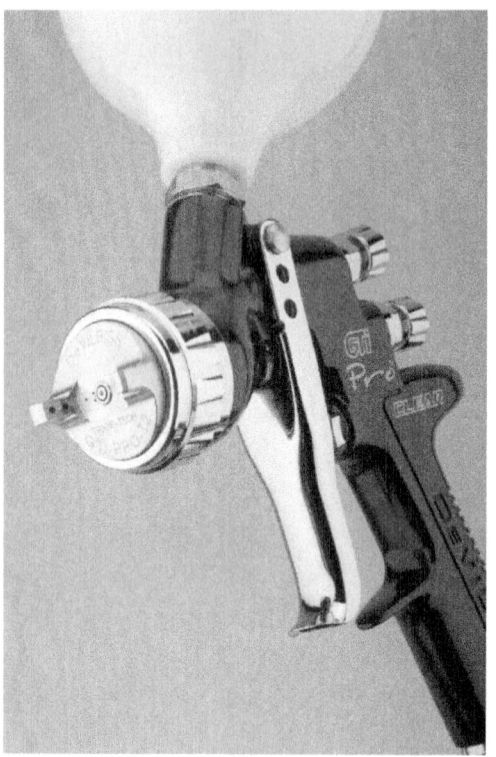

This type of gun has the paint in a container above the gun. The good thing about this is that the paint is drawn into the air flow by gravity which makes it work better. However, it is difficult to put down and you need a gun holder screwed to the wall to hold the gun when you are not spraying. Ideal in a spray booth situation but not very handy on site.

The suction feed gun

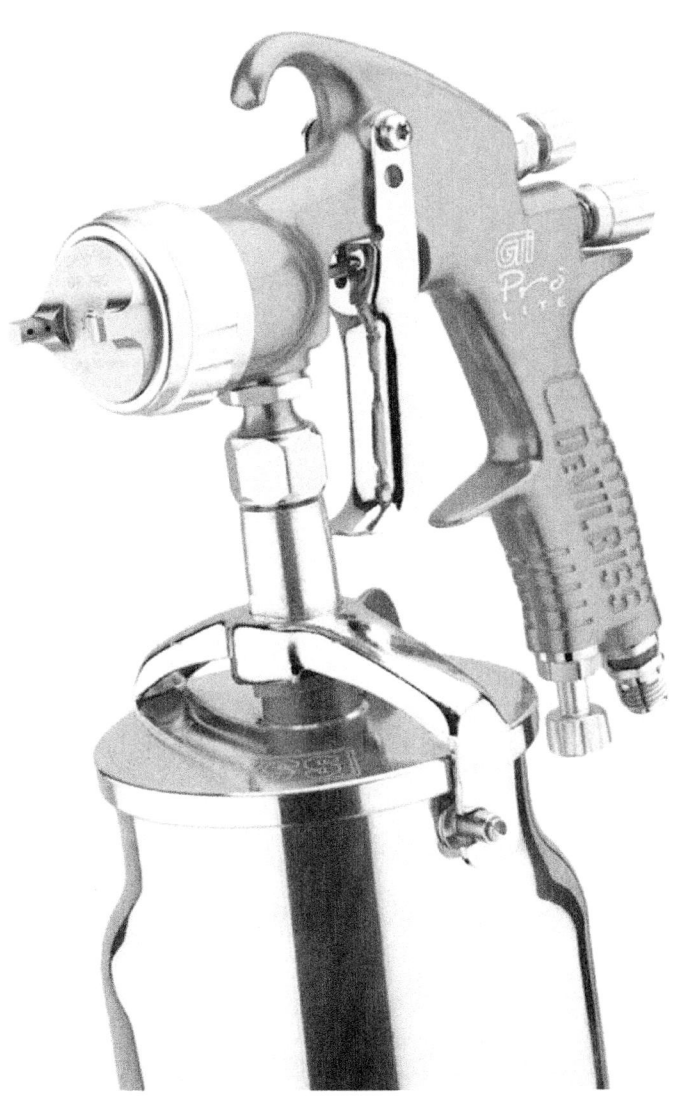

This type of gun has the paint in a pot below the gun. The paint is drawn up into the air stream by suction, the negative air pressure above the pot draws the paint up into the air stream.

The paint container is usually bigger than the gravity feed gun bit the gun does not feel as balanced as a gravity feed.

However, it is much easier to put down on the bench between spraying items.

Pressure feed

Finally, a pressure feed gun has a separate container for the paint and 2 hoses to the gun. This makes it lighter and easier to use when spraying. You can spray in tight spaces with ease and you can turn the gun upside down without any problems.

You can also hold larger quantities of paint in the pressure pot. These come in different sizes. Typically, 2 litres however you can get 5 or 10 litre pressure pots.

The pressure feed gun

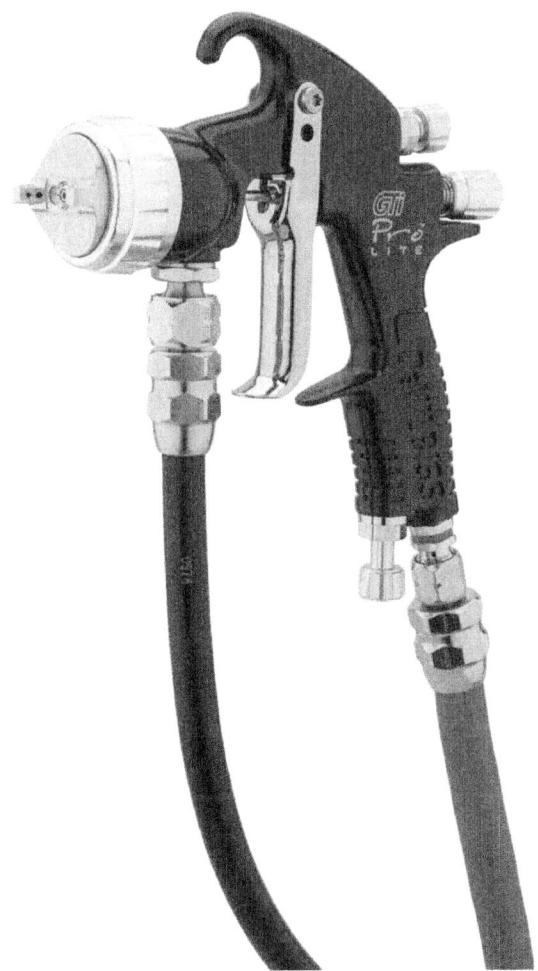

This can be a suction feed gun with the pot removed and the hose attached.

The pressure pot

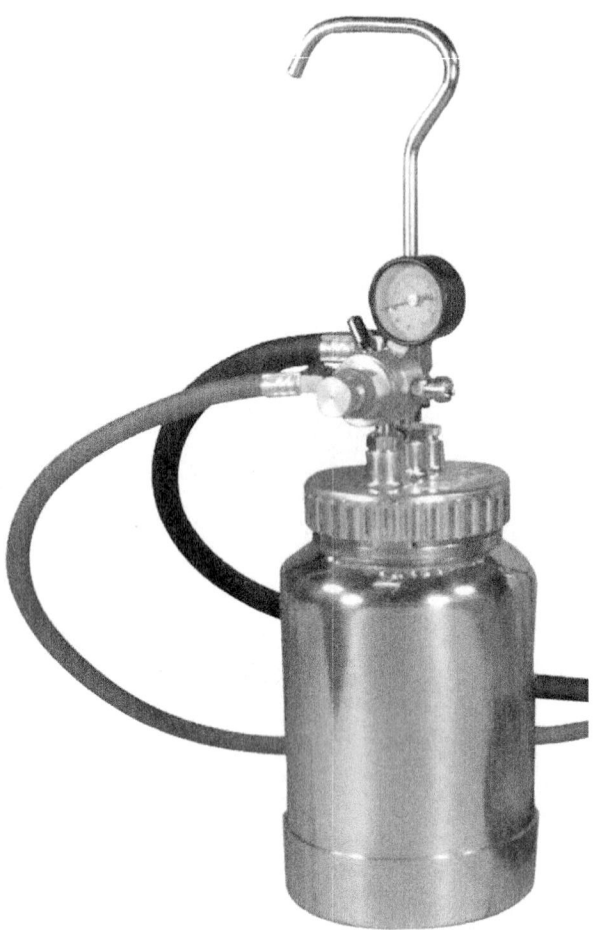

The pressure pot is attached to the compressor for air and the two hoses are attached to the gun. One for fluid and one for air. The air hose is attached to the handle of the spray gun.

Use a dry film thickness gauge

When we spray the sample panel, we are going to measure the film thickness. We will use the gauge shown below.

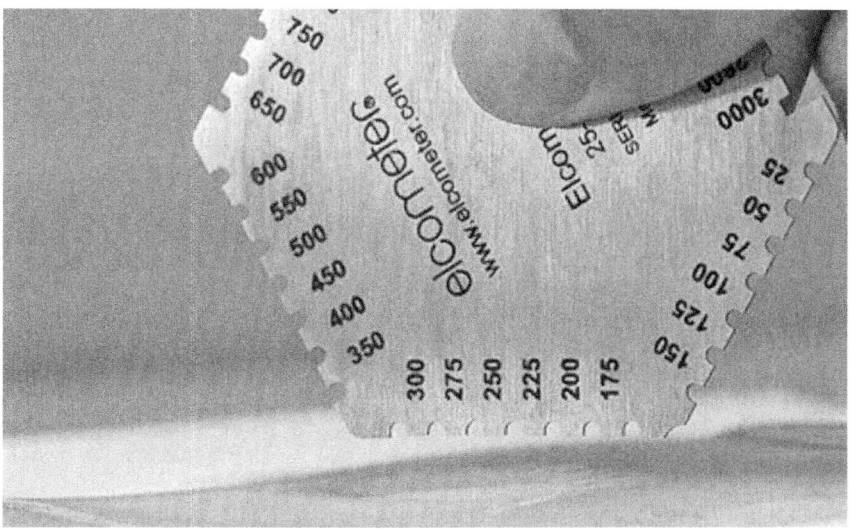

We are looking to get a wet film thickness of 100 microns. Mark 100 microns on the gauge with a sharpie pen and put the gauge into the wet coating. You will see how to read off the comb with an accurate reading.

Troubleshoot the equipment

There are not many things to go wrong with the HVLP turbine system. Here are some of the more common ones.

Paint not atomising properly, splattering
This is because the paint is too thick for the HVLP to atomise. You will need to thin the paint to a single cream consistency.

Paint not solid, only a thin film of paint
You need to turn the fluid control anti clockwise to let more fluid out of the fluid tip for the fan width setting.

Paint running on the surface
You need to turn the fluid control clockwise to reduce the amount of paint allowed through the gun.

Crescent moon shape fan pattern
This is a blockage on one of the air horns. Take the air cap off and give it a good clean.

Shut down and store the equipment

These are the steps needed to shut down and clean the equipment.

1. Switch off the turbine.

2. Disconnect the airline from the gun and then disconnect the paint container from the gun. Empty the paint back into the paint can. Wash out the paint container with warm water until it is clean.

3. Fill the paint container with warm water and re attach it to the gun. Attach the gun back onto the turbine and switch on. Spray the water through the gun to clear any paint from the system. This is easier with the air cap removed.

4. Once clean, switch off and take apart again. Dry off all the components.

5. It's worth screwing off the air cap and fluid tip just to make sure that these are really clean before putting the system away.

PAINTTECH TRAINING ACADEMY

INTRODUCTION TO AIRLESS SPRAYING

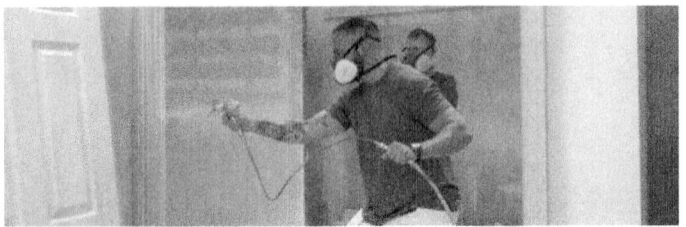

PRICE: £250 +VAT
(PER PERSON, MAXIMUM 6 IN A GROUP)

DURATION: 1 DAY

LOCATION: EDENBRIDGE, CREDITON, PRESTON, GLENROTHES & CASTLEBAR

You will cover all the main concepts such as:
- Basic Health & Safety
- Masking & De-masking
- Mindset & Objections
- Equipment set up & clean down
- Spray technique
- Different tips & accessories
- Common mistakes

COURSE CONTENT:

The course is mainly a practical day. Approximately 30% of the day is spent in the classroom and 70% is spent in the workshop.

You will spray a variety of surfaces, such as walls and ceilings, whilst using a basic set up, and then moving onto to different tip sizes for different scenarios, as well as the use of extension poles. You will also be taught how to set up your machine, change the paint and fully clean it out.

WEB - www.painttechtrainingacademy.co.uk   EMAIL - courses@painttechtrainingacademy.co.uk

PAINTTECH TRAINING ACADEMY

INTENSIVE AIRLESS SPRAYING

PRICE: £560 +VAT
(PER PERSON, MAXIMUM 6 IN A GROUP)

DURATION: 2 DAYS

LOCATION: EDENBRIDGE, CREDITON, PRESTON, GLENROTHES & CASTLEBAR

COURSE CONTENT:

The course is mainly practical, on the first day you will spend the morning in the classroom going through all the Health & Safety and theory aspects before moving into the workshop. Practical assessment takes place throughout the duration of the course and there is a short theory test at the end of day 2.

On successful completion of the course you will be awarded with a City & Guilds certificate, and you will also receive a digital credential which you can use on your website and across social media platforms.

You will cover all the main concepts such as:
- Basic Health & Safety
- Masking & De-masking
- Mindset & Objections
- Equipment set up & clean down
- Spray technique
- Different tips & accessories
- Common mistakes
- Products
- Tip sizes for use with trim
- Pressure/product/tip size combinations Systems

WEB - www.painttechtrainingacademy.co.uk   EMAIL - courses@painttechtrainingacademy.co.uk

PAINTTECH TRAINING ACADEMY

AIRLESS SPRAY PLASTER APPLICATION AND FINISHING

PRICE: £605 +VAT
(PER PERSON, MAXIMUM 5 IN A GROUP)

DURATION: 2 DAYS

LOCATION: EDENBRIDGE, CREDITON, PRESTON, GLENROTHES

On successful completion of the course you will be awarded with a City & Guilds certificate, and you will also receive a digital credential which you can use on your website and across social media platforms.

COURSE CONTENT:

The course is mainly a practical day. Approximately 10% of the day is spent in the classroom and 90% is spent in the workshop.

After being taught how to tape & joint, you will then spray walls and ceilings with the airless plaster, and then be shown how to turn this into an amazing level 5 finish.

You will cover all the main concepts such as:
- Products & suppliers
- Machines & tools
- Taping & Jointing
- External corners
- Internal corners
- Walls
- Ceilings
- Spatulas trowels

WEB - www.painttechtrainingacademy.co.uk   EMAIL - courses@painttechtrainingacademy.co.uk

PAINTTECH TRAINING ACADEMY
KITCHEN & FURNITURE ONSITE SPRAYING

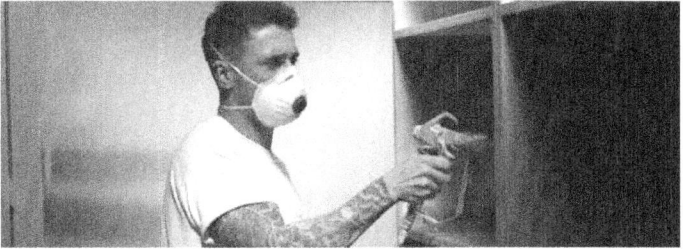

PRICE: £280 +VAT
(PER PERSON, MAXIMUM 5 IN A GROUP)

DURATION: 1 DAY

LOCATION: EDENBRIDGE, CREDITON, PRESTON, GLENROTHES & CASTLEBAR

You will cover all the main concepts such as:

- Products – water based, solvent based, acid cat, PU's and cellulose products
- Combination of workshop & on site set ups
- Pressures and products with the different machines
- Tips, tricks & masking techniques
- Spraying techniques
- Cleaning & maintenance
- Fault finding

Approved Training Organisation

COURSE CONTENT:

The course is a 100% practical day.

You will spray fitted furniture similar to that you would find on site, for example kitchen units & fitted shelving. You will be taught how to get an amazing finish on fitted furniture using various spray methods. This course is using the airless system it does not cover HVLP or compressor & you have to have completed the intro to spraying as a pre-requisite to this course.

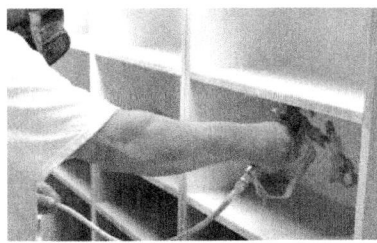

WEB - www.painttechtrainingacademy.co.uk   EMAIL - courses@painttechtrainingacademy.co.uk

PAINTTECH TRAINING ACADEMY

INTRODUCTION TO HVLP

PRICE: £285 +VAT
(PER PERSON, MAXIMUM 6 IN A GROUP)

DURATION: 1 DAY

LOCATION: EDENBRIDGE, CREDITON, PRESTON, GLENROTHES & CASTLEBAR

You will cover all the main concepts such as:
- Use of HVLP gravity fed & suction cup guns plus needle setting
- Use of pressure pots
- Conventional spraying using compressor
- Products
- Pressures and products with the different machines
- Spraying techniques
- Cleaning maintenance
- Fault finding

COURSE CONTENT:

The course is a 100% practical day.

This course is designed to show you how to get the best possible finish with your HVLP/LVLP or compressor set up. We look at all the different options, including pressure pots, compressors, HVLP machines, different needle sets and different types of guns.

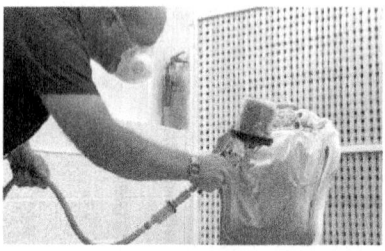

WEB - www.painttechtrainingacademy.co.uk   EMAIL - courses@painttechtrainingacademy.co.uk

PAINTTECH TRAINING ACADEMY
PAINTING USING HVLP EQUIPMENT

PRICE: £535 +VAT
(PER PERSON, MAXIMUM 6 IN A GROUP)

DURATION: 2 DAYS

LOCATION: EDENBRIDGE, CREDITON, PRESTON, GLENROTHES & CASTLEBAR

You will cover all the main concepts such as:
- Health & Safety
- Use of HVLP gravity fed & suction cup guns plus needle setting
- Use of pressure pots
- Conventional spraying using compressor
- Checking the suitability of previously prepared surfaces
- Pressures and products with the different machines
- Spraying techniques
- Cleaning & maintenance
- Fault finding

Approved Training Organisation

COURSE CONTENT:
The course is 20% classroom/theory and 80% practical training.

This course is designed to show you how to get the best possible finish with your HVLP/LVLP or compressor set up. We look at all the different options, including pressure pots, compressors, HVLP machines, different needle sets and different types of guns.

With 80% of this course over 2 days being practical you get a lot of time practicing your spray technique and learning how to correctly use the equipment.

WEB - www.painttechtrainingacademy.co.uk   EMAIL - courses@painttechtrainingacademy.co.uk

PAINTTECH TRAINING ACADEMY

PAPER HANGING INTRODUCTION

PRICE: £495 +VAT
(PER PERSON, MAXIMUM 6 IN A GROUP)

DURATION: 2 DAY

LOCATION: PRESTON
ROLLING OUT TO EDENBRIDGE, CREDITON, GLENROTHES & CASTLEBAR BY 2021.

COURSE CONTENT:
This is a two-day course aimed at people who have little or no experience of wallpapering. You will learn the basics including preparing the wall to receive wallpaper, the tools that would use and what to look for when buying wallpapering tools. You will also hang foundation papers to ceilings and walls. On the second day you will hang non-matching vinyl wallpaper to walls in a variety of situations. The emphasis will be on developing good skills that you can build on in the workplace.

- Adopt safe and healthy work practices, procedures and skills relating to the method/area of work.
- Use methods of calculating quantity, length, area and wastage associate with the method/procedure to hang wallcoverings.
- Check suitability of surfaces to receive wallpaper. This will involve looking at different surfaces and discussing how you would treat them before hanging wallpaper.
- Preparation of pastes and adhesives. You will look at a range of pastes and discuss what they are used for, this will include cellulose paste, starch pastes and ready mixed paste.
- Prepare and hang foundation paper, textured/relief finishing papers wallcoverings to walls.
- Work around electrical fittings and pipework.
- Safe use of access equipment, hand tools and associated equipment.

WEB - www.painttechtrainingacademy.co.uk   EMAIL - courses@painttechtrainingacademy.co.uk

PAINTTECH TRAINING ACADEMY

PAPER HANGING INTERMEDIATE

PRICE: £495 +VAT
(PER PERSON, MAXIMUM 4 IN A GROUP)

DURATION: 2 DAYS

LOCATION: PRESTON
ROLLING OUT TO EDENBRIDGE, CREDITON, GLENROTHES & CASTLEBAR BY 2021.

COURSE CONTENT:

This course is designed for people who have either done the paperhanging introduction and want to further improve their skills or someone who has done some wallpapering in industry and want to further their skills. The course will cover pattern papers and various types of wallpaper including non-woven, vinyl and traditional wallpapers. You will hang wallpaper in a range of settings including walls, ceilings, window reveals and a fireplace surround. You will be taught how to measure up these areas for wallpaper and how to handle different types of Pattern match.

- Adopt safe and healthy work practices, procedures and skills relating to the method/area of work
- Use methods of calculating quantity, length, area, and wastage associate with the method/procedure to hang wallcoverings
- Check suitability of surfaces to receive wallpaper.
- Preparation of pastes and adhesives.
- Prepare and hang the following: -Patterned vinyl, Non-woven, Traditional paper
- To the following surfaces: – Walls, Ceilings, Window reveal, Fireplace
- Work around electrical fittings
- Safe use of access equipment, hand tools and associated equipment

Approved Training Organisation

WEB - www.painttechtrainingacademy.co.uk   EMAIL - courses@painttechtrainingacademy.co.uk

PAINTTECH TRAINING ACADEMY

APPLYING PRINTED MURALS

PRICE: £325 +VAT
(PER PERSON. MAXIMUM 6 IN A GROUP)

DURATION: 1 DAY

LOCATION: PRESTON
ROLLING OUT TO EDENBRIDGE, CREDITON, GLENROTHES & CASTLEBAR BY 2021.

COURSE CONTENT:

This course will teach you how to incorporate murals into your decorating business. Installing murals is a fast growing and very profitable area of decorating. The course will build on existing paperhanging skills, if you have no experience wallpapering then you will have to do the paperhanging introduction first. The course will cover different types of murals including multi plate and one-piece murals. You will be taught what tools are needed and how to install the mural. You will be taught common problems that arise and also how to market the concept to the customer. You will work to apply different types of murals and gain an understanding of their strengths and weaknesses.

- Understanding different types of murals including multi plate and one-piece murals.
- Understanding how murals are created and considerations for images when creating a bespoke mural.
- Look at the tools and equipment needed to apply a mural.
- Preparation of the wall area. This will include how you would handle different surfaces and bring them to a standard to receive the mural.
- Understanding the different types of paste and which ones will be suitable for the application of a mural and why.
- Measuring up the wall area for ordering the mural.
- Preparing the work area for application of the mural.
- Applying a multi plate mural, considerations to be allowed for.
- Applying a one-piece mural.

WEB - www.painttechtrainingacademy.co.uk   EMAIL - courses@painttechtrainingacademy.co.uk

ESTIMATING FOR PAINTING & DECORATING (COMMERCIAL & DOMESTIC)

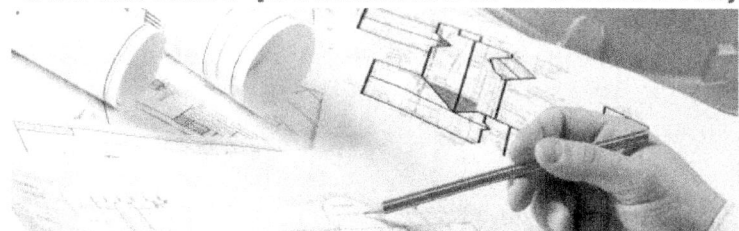

COURSE CONTENT:

This is a two-day course aimed at decorators who want to learn how to price their work correctly. The course assumes no previous knowledge of pricing and will start basic and build up your knowledge. The course will start by looking at some of the common pitfalls that decorators fall into when pricing their work.

Then the course will look at common pricing models that are widely used in the industry including a basic time and materials approach to a more sophisticated system that allows you to price off plans. The course will teach you how to calculate materials needed including paint and wallpaper. The course will help you to look at your own business and work out what your costs are, this is essential if you are going to price for work and make sure that you will make money.

Although the course is classroom based the majority of the course will be pricing activities and exercises. This will give you hands on experience of pricing real word jobs.

THE COURSE WILL COVER

- Basic maths, this includes working out areas of ceiling and walls. It will also look at how to calculate linear measurements such as skirting and architraves.
- Calculating your costs, this will include your overheads and labour costs.
- Calculating the quantities of materials needed for the contract. We will calculate both paint and wallpaper quantities.
- Pricing a simple job.
- Exploring budget revisions and how to handle them.
- Looking at pricing per square metre and what the current market rates are.
- Looking at "book" rates and how to use these in your business, also the advantages and disadvantages of book rates.
- Calculating a price from plans.

PRICE: £700 +VAT
(PER PERSON, MAXIMUM 10 IN A GROUP)

DURATION: 2 DAYS

LOCATION: PRESTON, EDENBRIDGE, CREDITON & GLENROTHES.

Approved Training Organisation

Fast and Flawless
A guide to airless spraying

This is a chatty guide to airless spraying for decorators, decorating students and anyone interested in spraying with an airless system.

The book covers all aspects of the airless sprayer including the components of the system, the different sprayers that are out there to buy and setting up the sprayer.

The book also covers topics such as types of sprayers, essential equipment, using the equipment, masking, PPE and masks, a bit about paint and finally what to do when it all goes wrong, spraying in the real world and common paint defects.

Fast and Flawless Pricing
A guide to pricing and business for decorators

Are you a decorator that struggles with pricing?
Have you just set up in business and are looking for some pointers?.

Are you an established business looking for some inspiration on how to move forward?

This chatty guide on pricing and business will gently guide you through the process of pricing a decorating job. It looks at the pitfalls of getting your pricing wrong and the advantages of having a good pricing system.

The book has been written by someone who has both been a decorator and taught decorating in a local college for most of his life.

Fast and Flawless Systems
A Decorators guide to planning and carrying out successful job

This book looks at systems for Decorators.

This book covers all types of systems from which paint to use on what surface to what order you should spray a room.

The book also covers aspects of decorating that you may or may not be aware of such as painting uPvc, training, funding and marketing.

If you have read the other two books already then this is one is a must read, if you haven't then this book is a great place to start.

Printed in Great Britain
by Amazon